DEAR MEN

Talitha Harrison

Copyright© 2021 by Talitha Harrison

All rights reserved. Per the U. S. Copyright Act of 1976, the scanning, uploading, and electronic sharing of any part of this book without the permission of the publisher constitute unlawful piracy and theft of the author's intellectual property. If you would like to use the material from the book (other than for review purposes), prior written permission must be obtained by contacting the publisher at **purethoughtspublishingllc@gmail.com**. Thank you for your support of the author's rights.

Pure Thoughts Publishing Company
2055 Gees Mills Rd., #316
Conyers, GA 30013
www.TalithaHarrison.com

The publisher is not responsible for websites or their content that is not owned by the publisher.

Printed in the United States of America.

ISBN 978-1-943409-71-6

I have learned that the things I have experienced in my life were not mistakes but were main events that placed me on the trajectory of purpose and destiny that was ordained for my life.

BY: TALITHA HARRISON

This book made me cry. It took me back to my childhood and how I grew up. It made me want to do more for my daughters and be a better father. I see differently now.

-R. Humes

Dear Men. When I read the beginning of the book, my thoughts were, if a man read this book and took the words to heart, what an amazing husband, 'boy' friend, brother, or sweetheart he would be. Talitha has a way of putting love and warmth into words. I would give this book to the men and boys in my family.

-Judge L. Tindal

This gem of a book reveals the fundamentals from the heart of a woman who has a burden to support men who are seeking practical ways to help mend or heal the brokenness we try to hide or covertly handle. Empowering men to be patient but intentional in mending, so we can live a real and holistic life.

-D. Walker

Dear Men is a thought-out, well provoked, wake-up call for the societal usurpation of the position, power and creation of the men in women's lives. It is rightfully, honestly transparent in reminding Dear Men to rethink how to approach and treat real women of today. The honesty connects a raw exposed hunger of emotion to men who need to wake up to walk in their purpose. It is a reminder of their role in creation. It is a plea for the release of those bound. Dear Men…it's time! A wonderful read for the Dear Men in your lives!

-Dr. Tia Buchanan, LPC, LAC, LPCS, EMDRC, M.A., M.S., DMin. Acorns n Bones OMC

Acknowledgments

Thanks to the support of my family, I can now give my pain a voice and bring healing to so many.

I would like to thank my older brothers Willie Martin, Jr., affectionately known as Junior, and Perry Martin who besides my father, Willie Martin, Sr., were the first men in my life that loved me unconditionally. These men nurtured me, protected me as well as corrected me. Thank you, Junior, for taking me to see my first movie at the theatre. That was really monumental for me. All these years later, I still enjoy that movie. Thank you, Perry, for teaching me to sing in perfect pitch in the background as you sang lead, and for choosing me to be in your first music video. I had a lot of fun making it. Junior, you had a part in that vocal training too.

To my younger sisters and brother, Stacey (Ne Ne) Bullock, Alexis (Demore) Wilson, Arnell Martin, and Ashley Martin, I am so grateful for all the love mommy had to share in expanding our family. Because of you all, I know love on a whole different level.

To my editors, Tracey Dwight, Gina McGowan Cade and Chance Douglas (my late in the midnight hour editor), thank you all for your time, patience, support, encouragement, advice and expertise.

To Pure Thoughts Publishing Company, thank you for your patience and showing me that this was achievable.

Dedication

I dedicate this book to my parents, Willie and Sallie Mae Martin, who live in my heart daily. It is because of you two, I have compassion and the heart to serve those that are hurting. Thank you, daddy and mommy, for always loving and supporting me. I love you both so much and miss the two of you immensely!

To my daughters, Shaleytha, Taleysha, Tachae, and my granddaughter Jaylah, know that I love you all unconditionally.

There are times when we are going through situations and circumstances, and we do not understand them at the time. However, as life begins to unfold it starts to make sense. It is at that time, understanding comes and your why's are answered.

As purpose, destiny, and wealth transpire, you will then realize and know it was necessary. It was part of the plan, to land you where you were called.

Life hasn't been perfect. At times, it's been extremely difficult and painful. However, I am a firm believer that you must give your pain a voice. In doing so, your pain will be turned into purpose, bringing healing to yourself and so many others.

Each of you young ladies are filled with wisdom beyond your years. I know you will all do great and excel in life.

I am so proud of you all.

Table of Contents

Acknowledgments v

Dedication vi

Foreword 8

INTRODUCTION 10

DEAR MEN, ...15

BACK DOWN MEMORY LANE 18

THE PROTECTOR AND THE PROVIDER 25

HEAL FOR US ALL! 30

TO MY DEAR MAN 36

REAL MEN MEND 39

About the Author 42

Foreword

Talitha and her newly acclaimed book, *Dear Men*, took me down a journey, and it hit me in so many areas. *Dear Men* is an inspiration, a savior for many people and relationships. It will be an eye-opener, a book that encourages, and touches so many lives; especially a lot of brothers. The author is speaking so much truth. I saw myself in this book. I can identify with so much from *Dear Men* because I have been through a lot of the experiences that are spoken about within its pages.

When I read this book, it touched me in so many areas as if it was talking directly to me. This is the perfect time for *Dear Men*.

I see conversations happening about *Dear Men* in barbershops, clubs, locker rooms, lounges, wherever men convene.

Dear Men has opened my eyes in many areas and is sure to open quite a few more, in many communities, countries, and cultures.

Gary McFarland

INTRODUCTION

INTRODUCTION

This book started as a conversation that was birthed out of so much pain.

Men, I can't begin to tell you how necessary you are, and how much worth you have on this earth. You are so valued, respected, and loved. More than anything, respect is required to be given to you from all. If it were not for you, we would not be here. From the beginning of time, you have been the builder of strong foundations, protectors, and providers. Then something happened.

I grew up with two older brothers. One brother is ten years older than me, and the other brother is seven years older. They would often do their own thing, whatever that was. I was so much younger, I stayed mostly with my mom on her days off. However, because my mom worked a full-time job and my dad worked two jobs I was left in the care of my brothers, who showed me much love and protection.

I must say, as I smile while typing this, they also showed me how to fight. When I say fight, I mean physically. My oldest brother went to Karate school, so I would get the high kicks, the low kicks, the side kicks, and the roundhouse kicks. He was kind enough to show me how to block some of them. You know he had to get a few in for his kicks. Yes, the pun is intended.

Then there was my other brother, the slow smooth walking one that wore the three-piece gabardine suits, platform shoes with the wide brim hats, that the few female friends I had growing up were scared of. They would ask, "Is your brother a pimp?" I would say, "No!" while laughing. They would then say, "Oh, I thought he was a pimp because of the way he dressed." I would just laugh. Well, this brother would hit and pick on me for the fun of it. One thing was for sure, if he found out I was fighting guys or if guys were harassing me, he always came to my rescue.

I must say, when I did fight, I was so proud to throw my punches because my brothers taught me how not to fight like a girl which was their words, not mine. Guys were always impressed when they saw me throw as the closed fist turns before it gets to the person's face punches. They would always say the same. "You don't fight like a girl" would be the common statement with guys. And in my head, I'd be smiling saying, "Yeah, thanks to my brothers." I would at times give my brothers the credit verbally.

Even though I was their punching and kicking bag, I love my brothers to this day! They have always been fun to be around. Even now, we sit back and tell stories about it. We were a very close-knit family, my father, mother, two brothers, and myself.

Later on in life, another brother was born, and I can proudly say that I was very instrumental in raising him to be the kind-hearted and gentleman he is today because my mother passed away when he was nine years old. I have sisters also, but because this book is for men, I'll talk about them in the next book.

I grew up hanging around my male cousins Jerome, Gary, and Benjamin who were my best friends. Between my older brothers and my cousins, they have somewhat shaped and formed my life to be extremely comfortable with men. After a while, I found myself having great dialogue with men. I worked in a male-dominated establishment. I would find myself in Q&A conversations with men quite often. We've become great listeners to one another. To date, I find men to be so easy to converse with. Intimate relationships with men were different. They were more challenging.

My cousins, Jerome and Gary, are now deceased. Gary died as a victim of a homicide and his brother Jerome died due to health complications. According to an article written by Ined, Institut National D'Etudes Demographiques, "The number of men and women in the world is roughly equal, though men hold a slight lead with 102 men for 100 women (in 2020). More precisely, out of 1,000 people, 504 are men (50.4%) and 496 are women (49.6). For every 100 girls, 106 boys are born, but males have a higher risk of dying than females both in childhood and adult ages. So, at a certain age, the numbers of men and women even out. In France, this occurs at age 25. Beyond this age, women outnumber men, and the numerical difference between the two sexes increases with age." Their source was from the United Nations, Department of Economic and Social Affairs, Population Division (2019). World Populations Prospects 2019, customs data acquired via website.

Some of the reasons why women begin to outnumber men as the ages increase is because male suicides outnumber female suicides. Homicide and suicide are among the top causes of death among males. Other factors to take into consideration, are the lifespan of women being longer, and oftentimes, the lack of males taking care of their mental health as well as their physical health. Research shows that men who are clinically depressed are at a greater risk of coronary artery disease.

Do you believe that love, holding, touching, healing, expressions of affection, feeling safe enough to open up to respectful and gainful communication with the one woman that's right for you can change such a negative outcome?

Men, we need you. Not only do we need you, but we also want you in our lives. Only you can be a king or a prince. Without you, we wouldn't have a queen, our little princesses, or our little princes that will carry your name and legacy. You are created in the perfect image of a man. We do not want to do life without you.

Do you think if I hold you right, touch you right, hear you right, listen to you right would help or at least be a good start?

Do you think finding the right one is difficult or is finding someone you feel you can trust is even more difficult?

I believe with all my heart that if you continue to read, we will be able to figure some of these matters out and things will become a little clearer. I hope writing this book will begin to open the awareness of men and women alike and bring healing to both.

DEAR MEN,

DEAR MEN,

Men, we need you. Not only do we need you, we also want you in our lives. It bothers me to see a great portion of the male species deceived and buy into a lie. I know you were taught things like; men should not cry; you have to be tough, and don't be a wimp, or a punk. Along with other lies like, don't put all your eggs in one basket; you always need a backup, a just-in-case woman or one in the hole; every man needs more than just one woman, etc., you get what I'm saying. You are so much greater than the lies. Of course, this does not apply to all men. I know because I have brothers and some of my best friends were men. Some believed the lies, some didn't.

These lies are getting so many of our men out of position, leaving so many women vulnerable and unprotected. We are left as prey, to be devoured by whatever is lurking to violate, steal, and kill our spirits, our lives, and the spirits of our little children.

Because of the actions that are being perpetrated by some men, many women refer to them as womanizers, players, and dogs. Even though dogs are precious animals to us human beings, we should not be referencing you as such. There should be a higher regard for our men. A few indiscretions made by some, can leave a number of women with a bitter taste in their mouth, asking, 'Where are the real men?' as if men of integrity and good character are an extinct and rare species.

You possess the ability to assist in making me whole or to break me into pieces. You are wise and created in the perfect image of a man. I don't want to do life without you.

BACK DOWN MEMORY LANE

BACK DOWN MEMORY LANE

I can remember being in elementary and junior high school. The little boys would send the little girls notes in class asking, "Do you want to go with me?" or "Do you want to be my girlfriend?" "Check yes, no, or maybe."

At times the boys would send their friends to let the girls know they were interested in them and would inquire if the feeling was mutual. It was flattering being one of those little girls. We didn't know to be sassy and ask, "Go with you where?" We would just respond by checking one of those boxes with the choices they gave us. I remember once in junior high school receiving one of those notes. I gladly checked "yes" while blushing. Then he said to me, "Don't tell nobody," and I responded, "Okay" with my beautiful smile and my perfect white teeth. Back then, I didn't think anything of his request to keep it a secret. But nowadays, that request wouldn't go over so well. Neither would the paper request for me to be your girlfriend.

Times have changed, we've grown up and both younger and older people are more straightforward in their requests, and it requires much more than a pen and paper. Now as adults, we can look back at those days and realize life seemed so simple then, but for many, it wasn't simple at all.

Now to you men that have lived long enough to form your thoughts, as you evolved into an adult man, you began to experience different things and see some things differently.

Let me take some of you to what could be considered your now, and for others, your pleasant past. Do you remember going to church as an adult and seeing those adorable little girls that you smiled and waved at from one pew to the next on Sunday mornings? Perhaps it was the ones in your community that you would see outside playing, or at a family function?

How about you, sir? Do you remember those little girls that you were fortunate enough to raise in your home because you and your wife only had boys, or maybe you were not able to produce your own biological children?

Initially, you didn't want to take in any more children to raise in your household that were not yours. However, once you did, you fell in love with them. At first, you were uncertain as to what to do and how to raise them because you had never raised girls. It wasn't long before you realized that, yeah, you loved your biological sons, but on the other hand, these girls were even more special than the boys. You never wanted to spank them because you didn't want to do anything to hurt them. You took them to and from daycare and school.

Everything you did in your personal life before receiving these precious beauties, suddenly ceased. You gave it all up for them. You changed your work schedule to accommodate those little girls because they needed you. The moment you knew they weren't feeling well, you would stop what you were doing, even if it meant leaving work early to rush to the school and pick them up. To look at their small, pitiful, sickly faces and know that some discomfort was causing them hurt and pain, was so heart-wrenching that it would tear you up inside. Sometimes seeing them suffer was so unbearable, you would do anything and everything you could to make them feel better. You just couldn't wait to see a smile on their faces again because when they smiled, it warmed your heart and made you smile.

The thought of them being hurt, or anyone hurting your baby girls would make you irate. There was nothing anyone could say to remove the thought of you wanting to bring harm to anyone that would even think about hurting your little girls. You wanted to rescue them from a place of devastation and harm to return them to that place of peace, serenity, and happiness. Once that was achieved, then you too would be at peace and in a happy place.

When you first received them, they were undernourished, nervous, very scared, and lost. You did everything within your power to nourish them and feed them natural food for physical sustenance. You also provided them with your reassuring words, your dedication, your support, your protection, and your love.

What about the daughters that came from your very own loins, your seed that you helped conceive? Oh, how much you loved, comforted, protected, and made them feel secure! They knew they were the apple of their daddy's eye. The worth you are to your girls far outweighs any boyfriend she shall ever have.

Some little girls have not been that fortunate. Sometimes their daddy isn't present, nor has he ever been there for those precious little ones, to let them know how special they are and how they deserve to be loved and adored. Therefore, they grow up looking for what they never had. They become very vulnerable while unprotected. They are looking for this love and adoration in other men, but oftentimes end up in the arms of the wrong man.

Then some are empty, in search of something, but they don't know what. Resulting in them having low self-esteem, thinking they're not beautiful enough, walking around with their heads hung down, their thoughts low, and their decisions even lower.

Just as fate would have it, some man with wrong intentions notices her low self-esteem as if it is written across her forehead, preys on her, manipulating her into thinking that he cares. He then uses her lowliness to capitalize for his selfish gain.

In some cases, once upon a time, these precious darlings were doted over and spoiled. Everyone used to be drawn in when that baby girl looked at them with those bright eyes. Later, down the line, their bright eyes grew dim. The twinkle in their eyes was gone.

What about the precious little girls? My heart goes out to the ones that have been sexually abused from infancy through adulthood. Thinking about the lady up the block who was abandoned, left to struggle and raise those beautiful daughters alone.

She was single and thought this man who portrayed himself to be her knight in shining armor would be her happily ever after. Instead, he put her family on the road to disaster because he knew that their daddy wasn't around. What most people didn't know was that her children were being molested and raped. This atrocity had turned those little ladies and their mother's lives upside down. Their life went from mom going to work, rushing at the end of the workday to pick one daughter up from daycare, another from the babysitter, with the others old enough to walk home from school to years of sleepless nights, doctor appointments, counseling sessions and group meetings at the local organization for children of sexual abuse.

This was such a horrible life and an unfortunate situation that this family endured. Of course, no one knew. They couldn't tell anyone except the counselor about the trauma, the rejection, the abandonment, the abuse, the lack of true love, affection, appreciation, and adoration from their father.

For many years following, maybe even the rest of their lives, these young ladies would continue to struggle with nightmares, night terrors, day terrors, and graphic scenes in the memories of their now traumatized minds. Not only were they depressed, but they had broken hearts, spirits, and broken thoughts. These poor broken young ladies. Can you imagine how difficult this must have been on the mother?

If people knew, they would probably have been the talk of the town. That stigma would have been the hot topic from preschool throughout their adult lives. They weathered that storm, which could have been the hardest, most difficult time in their life, bleakly seeing that there was a light at the end of the tunnel. Hoping and praying, that the rest of their lives would be as smooth-sailing as possible, because, after all of that, they really couldn't take anything else. If they were to allow someone to come into their lives, they would be looking for great companionship, trust, true love, protection, and security.

Little girls are the cutest, most precious beings to me. Such innocence, playing, living out different phases of their current and future lives as they see it, or maybe as they would like it to be through their dolls.

Some little girls grew up with a lot of love and security. Some grew up with love in the absence of security. Some grew up with security and no love, and some little girls grew up with neither. Some grew up with various types of abuse. No matter which scenario was prevalent in their past lives, one thing these young ladies are in search of is to be loved and to feel secure in a healthy relationship.

THE PROTECTOR AND THE PROVIDER

THE PROTECTOR AND THE PROVIDER

The truth is, as I said earlier, men are supposed to provide for and protect their women and children. For some of us, men are supposed to take the leadership role in our lives. Not a "do as I say" role, but instead a "grab my hand, as I reach out for yours, and come with me as I lead you by example, with you by my side" role. Some of us are okay with you leading if we can trust you to lead us in the right direction. Instead, so many of our men are giving attention to other things. Some are too busy chasing multiple women as opposed to focusing on the one they have. Some of the lies I mentioned earlier are pushing so many men out of position, leaving women vulnerable and unprotected. We are left as prey, to be devoured by whatever is lurking to violate, steal, kill our spirits, destroy our lives, and the spirits of our little children. Protect us. Provide for us.

As women, we need you to show us kindness, patience, understanding, empathy, respect, and compassion. Practicing emotional support is a necessity that requires maturity. If I can just get commitment, faithfulness, honesty, sensitivity, companionship, and partnership from you, there is nothing that I wouldn't do for you.

I'm not asking for anything that shouldn't exist in a relationship. The things I am requesting should be the basis of our relationship without me begging and pleading for them.

Men you were created to be the head, our provider, our protector, and in some cases, our burden bearer to carry the load. When you are not in your role in the relationship, it places an undue amount of stress on us women. We were created to be by your side, not alone carrying the load that we were not intended to carry. It causes an enormous amount of tension to our existence and our health.

Let's take for instance the single mother raising your child, and you're not there in any capacity, being present as you should. She would then have to make provision for the children at almost any cost. It took two to make this beautiful human being from the start, and it takes two to continue to bring a complete balance to him/her.

You can say you don't have the money for food, daycare, or whatever the child might need, but the mother would have to come up with it. She has no choice. If there is a situation that arises in school, the mother has to show up. If your child is being bullied, the mother has to be the protector and carry this load by herself. When the child has homework and needs help, the mother has to be there. Protect the mother from being overwhelmed and provide for the child as only a father can provide; mentally, emotionally, physically, and psychologically.

What if there are multiple children? Think about how much this can affect the mother. Sometimes, it's so stressful it makes the body physically ill. Your body can only take on so much before it breaks down. The mind operates the same way.

I have known women to get so overwhelmed that they contemplated suicide. If it had not been for the children they sacrificed everything for, and knowing that if they weren't around, there wouldn't be anyone to care for and raise their children, some would have committed suicide. Trust me I know, I have been there and so have many other women out there. A man can affect the MENtality of the woman negatively, by not being there to support, provide and protect.

How much do you think a woman can take before you, the man, break her down? We have given you our whole heart. Now, not by any means am I telling you that all women are perfect but know that there are plenty of good ones around, and if you look right in front of you, or on either side of you, you may be looking right at her.

Men, I'm not trying to beat you up or tear you down, but instead, I want to build you up and encourage you back into position. Remember in the beginning, I stated, this doesn't apply to all of you, but there are some of you it does apply to.

I remember asking a woman I know who went through and stood by her husband throughout his numerous affairs, embarrassing situations and never left him, "How can you deal with all of that? I can't stay in a relationship where there is betrayal, unfaithfulness, and infidelity." Her answer was very simple. She responded, "They all come with mess!" Believe it or not, that helped me, but not enough to continue to stay in a relationship and take their "mess!"

What I realized is, yes, quite a few come with mess, but they have never thought or cared about how much "mess" she has already fought through and endured.

Let's look at this for a minute, you come with your mess, the one before you came with their mess, and the one before him came with his mess. What you don't realize is, your woman's mental capacity cannot take all of that while being expected to operate at optimum functionality and peak performance in every area of her life. There will be a breakdown in performance that is destined to show up.

All of the unnecessary letdowns, disappointments, betrayals, manipulation, and lies that the woman has endured can affect the chemical balance in her brain. It can also, cause various types of sicknesses, illnesses, and diseases in her body. This is why it is so important for you not to bring "mess" when you enter her life because you don't know if she can take anything else. It can kill her or show up as a mental meltdown, nervous breakdown, cancer, autoimmune disease, or other things.

Some men like to look at a woman when she has reached her breaking point, call her crazy and not accept responsibility for their actions that perhaps has pushed her to the point of no return. Could it be that she loves you, but doesn't have any more mental space for any more mess in her life?

Could it be that she keeps giving love a try but has been depleted of her substance and the very essentials that kept her together?

If you know you are not going to do right by someone, please leave her alone. You don't know where they are emotionally, mentally, or physically. You don't know what they were presented with in life before you entered their life.

There were times I had to walk away loving him until my emotions caught up with my move.

Just because she looks strong, beautiful, and well put together, it doesn't mean that she is inside. Her heart has been broken into a million pieces. Remember, many of us are used to doing what we have to do for ourselves, our children and looking good as we do it, while hiding our tears in the process.

I won't even get into the sometimes perpetual cycle of a young lady raising a son on her own, who never had her father in her life to father her, or show a real representation of a responsible male figure. I can't say it enough, we need you to take your position back and walk with purpose and destiny, fulfilling your assignment in life. No broken places in your relationship and no missing pieces.

HEAL FOR US ALL!

HEAL FOR US ALL!

Men, please heal! Yes, please heal if you have experienced a relationship with a woman who was broken and also in need of healing due to her past. Maybe, she didn't recognize your value or your worth and didn't give you the respect you deserved. It could have been your mother who didn't realize the greatness she gave birth to, or possibly, it was a woman you had a relationship with in your past. Perhaps, that woman lied to you and betrayed your trust. Maybe your story is somewhat like mine. I recognize hurt when I see it.

Please take the time to do whatever is necessary to get the healing you need before you move on with me. Don't make me pay for what has happened to you in your past, because I'm not her. So, don't punish me because some other woman hurt you. I didn't do it. I didn't lie to you. I didn't cheat on you.

And no, all women are not the same. I may be the one that sees your worth, gives you the respect that is due to you, and the one that is going to stand by your side. Just give me a fair chance. But, you can't do that if you don't allow yourself to heal. I may be what you need, but you have to be all in, not just give me fragmented pieces of yourself. I will love you. I will respect, adore, admire, and appreciate you.

You won't see that I'm the one for you if the woman that hurt you in the past still has power and control over your thoughts and actions. That means her actions are still affecting you to this day.

It's okay to cry and be truthful with your feelings. We need our little boys and young men to know that as well. Please forgive and heal, then move on. If you don't, in some cases, it will leave you with feelings of low self-esteem, questioning your worth and putting you on a path of targeting women that you feel are weak, or battling with low self-esteem issues themselves. As a result, leaving women in pain, crying and pondering, *"Why did you take advantage of my low self-esteem, or what you deemed as my unattractiveness? Was it just to use me as an object of yours so I can treat you like a king, build you up, worship the ground you walk on, and you do not reciprocate? Instead, you tread on my heart, my soul and break me into even more pieces. It's as if I'm your enemy and you're going to make me pay for all the wrong that was done to you in your life. Or are you going to keep this wall up that you call your guard to keep me from getting in your heart, out of fear of being hurt again?"* You are not giving me or us a fair chance. You are robbing yourself of one of the best experiences you can have in life.

In my nature to nurture you, peace, where did it go?

I lost myself in trying to fix and repair you. I found out you were broken, and I couldn't fix you, I couldn't put you together. I tried my best though. So much so, that I made fixing you my purpose in my broken state. Then when you tore me down, even more, you looked at me and didn't like what you saw. So, you spit on me, you disrespected me with your words and your actions. Then you rejected me. You abandoned me. You cheated on me. You lied to me. Not to mention, you lied on me. You coming to me, in the beginning, was a lie within itself. Protecting and providing, you did not do.

You look back at me; my eyes are no longer big and bright. They are now small and dull. My complexion is dry, the smile is gone. But I'm only what you created.

All I wanted to do was love you, support you and help you be the best version of you that you can be. While doing that, I was hopeful you would make me happy and whole, feeling safe and secure. Maybe, I experienced that feeling growing up and was looking for it again. Then, there is a great chance I haven't experienced it but wanted it so bad; I searched for it my whole life.

Men, I believe in you. I need you. We need you. Know that you have within you the power to help heal me and make me whole. When you heal, I heal. Together we can do anything.

Look at me again. That little girl is still here. I want to come out and play every now and then. I want to feel safe. I'm scared, and I want to know if I can trust you. I want to know that you will protect me and always have my back. I want to know that you will be honest with me and never lie to me. Oh yeah, and please don't cheat on me. If I can get these things from you, then I'll know that I am secure. I can then blossom while walking with my head held high if I know that you respect me and will never place anyone above me. You see, I never wanted to compete with anyone for your love. I just want to love you in peace.

Choose a woman, don't use one. Set her in the place to be the advantage, don't take advantage. After you have chosen her, please cherish, provide, protect her and your relationship. Give her your all.

Men, walk in your rightful place as providers, protectors, strong builders with dignity, integrity, and character. Provide us with the love, protection, security, the strong foundation of relationship and family built on truth.

TO MY DEAR MAN

TO MY DEAR MAN

I was already betrayed. I was already cheated on. I was already lied to. I was already manipulated. I was already taken advantage of. I was violated. I barely made it to this point in life.

Depending on my journey in life, and how I respond to it, I'm going to run in your arms, or run away from you - both for the same reasons.

I'm scared! I'm looking for safety and security; not to be harmed, physically, emotionally, or mentally; not to ever be broken again – not anymore.

You see, you can either make me smile or make me cry. You can make me shine or dim my light. You can lift me up or tear me down. You can hold me and support me, or you can push me out there to figure it out on my own. You can love me, or you can hate me. You can shatter me, or you can embrace me.

But know this, before you met me, I was already abandoned and rejected by my father, mother, or both. I was already abandoned and rejected by the man I loved before you, and please don't punish me for that.

I was already undernourished, molested, raped (a few times), emotionally taken advantage of, and abused, mentally taken advantage of, and abused, physically taken advantage of, and abused.

My heart had already been walked on, trampled on, crushed, and shattered into many pieces. As a result of all I've been through, I attempted to take my own life. I thought about suicide many times.

You remember those little girls we talked about in the beginning, right? The ones you raised. The ones sitting in the pews of the church. The ones that were scared, undernourished, nervous, rejected and abandoned. The ones you were responsible for. Remember? The ones you did everything for, to make them feel safe and secure. Once you won their trust, you never wanted to do anything to lose it.

You nurtured them until they weren't nervous anymore. They weren't starved for food or attention. You covered them and protected them. When they called you, you were right there at the sound of their voice. When you heard them cry, you ran to their rescue to fix what was ailing them. You could not fathom hurting them or the thought of anyone else hurting them.

Yes, you remember them. Well, those little girls are in every woman you meet. Yes, I am that little girl.

REAL MEN MEND

REAL MEN MEND

So, Dear Men, when you see me in the supermarket, the mall, the drugstore, at work, or in the church, and if you can't say to me, "Let me wipe those tears from your eyes, the ones I don't see, but I know are there. Or, let me mend your broken heart that I know has been broken many times before you met me." Then, don't even stop to say "Hi," just continue to walk on by.

Getting my number is not an option. I don't need another disappointment in my life and cannot afford another heartbreak because this one may take me over the edge. I may have a mental meltdown. This could be the one that may send me to a mental institution, cause heart disease, stroke, or suicide. The stress could expedite any underlying illness that could cost my life. If you need time to fix yourself, then take all the time you need. I'll be here.

And in the event, I did give you my number, and our relationship faces a few challenges or temptation arises to cheat on me, betray me, or look in my eyes to lie to me, look at me again and see the little girl in me that just wants to be held, protected, cherished, loved and made whole. I too want to give that to you.

If you choose not to hold, protect, cherish, love, and bring healing to me and our relationship becomes toxic and unhealthy, let's make the mature decision and walk away. Let me go.

Please, please, don't bring any more hurt to my life. Life in general comes with a lot of hurt and pain. Sometimes, it was so much hurt, I didn't know if I was ever going to heal again, but somehow, I did. Please, if you can't make me happy, don't hurt me. If you can't make me smile, don't make me frown.

So, Men, before you come to me, know that I have already been broken and let down. I've already been lied to, betrayed and abused. Know that if I invite you into my life, I have already experienced, and have been exposed to some, if not all of these transgressions before meeting you.

You can trust me; you can be vulnerable with me. Deep inside, we are longing for you, the real, true, authentic man. You are so valuable. We need you. Your children need you to talk with them, to listen and hear them, to hug them, to love and care for them, and so does your community. Please, just remember who you are and all the great responsibilities that come with who you are.

And for those of you who are already handling yours, thank you!

I appreciate you! There is one thing I would like to request your assistance in. Please take the time to encourage our younger and older men to not accept the lie that has tried to infiltrate them throughout generations; that lie that makes them run away and neglect their responsibility to their women and their children, but embrace us instead. Love us instead.

Our lives are so much better with you in them. Our children's lives are so much greater, and they are healthier because you are committed to doing your part and being there while supporting their dreams and endeavors to succeed in life.

Please walk in your rightful place. We need you.

Thank you, men, for hearing my heart.

I love you.

Respectfully always…

About the Author

Talitha Martin Harrison is a mother, a transformational life coach, a retired law enforcement Captain from NYC Department of Corrections - Rikers Island, who currently works as a Victim's Advocate at the District Attorney's Office and is very active in her community.

Harrison has counseled hundreds of hurting men and women in need of love and guidance throughout most of her life and career.

She has coached, empowered, mentored, and shifted the mindset of so many people of all ages, youth to adults, globally.

She is the founder of four non-profit organizations.

Harrison's passion to help others is undeniable and has birthed many platforms to address the heartbreaking reality and concerns of the community and the nation as a whole. As a result, Ms. Harrison writes from a place of vulnerability and transparency from her personal experiences of trials and triumphs as well as her pure love for hurting people everywhere.

www.DearMenOfficial.com
www.TalithaHarrison.com

www.ingramcontent.com/pod-product-compliance
Lightning Source LLC
Chambersburg PA
CBHW060508050426
42451CB00009B/877